city sounds

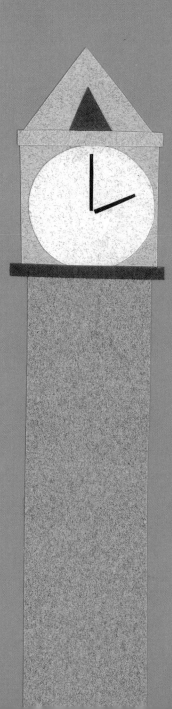

city sounds

by Rebecca Emberley

Little, Brown and Company
Boston   Toronto   London

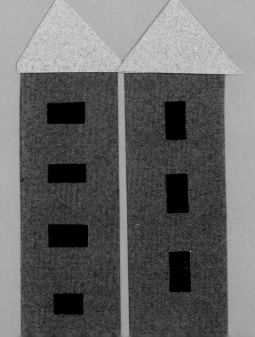

First edition

Library of Congress Catalog Card Number 88-81191

10 9 8 7 6 5 4 3 2

Published simultaneously in Canada
by Little, Brown & Company (Canada) Limited

Printed in Hong Kong

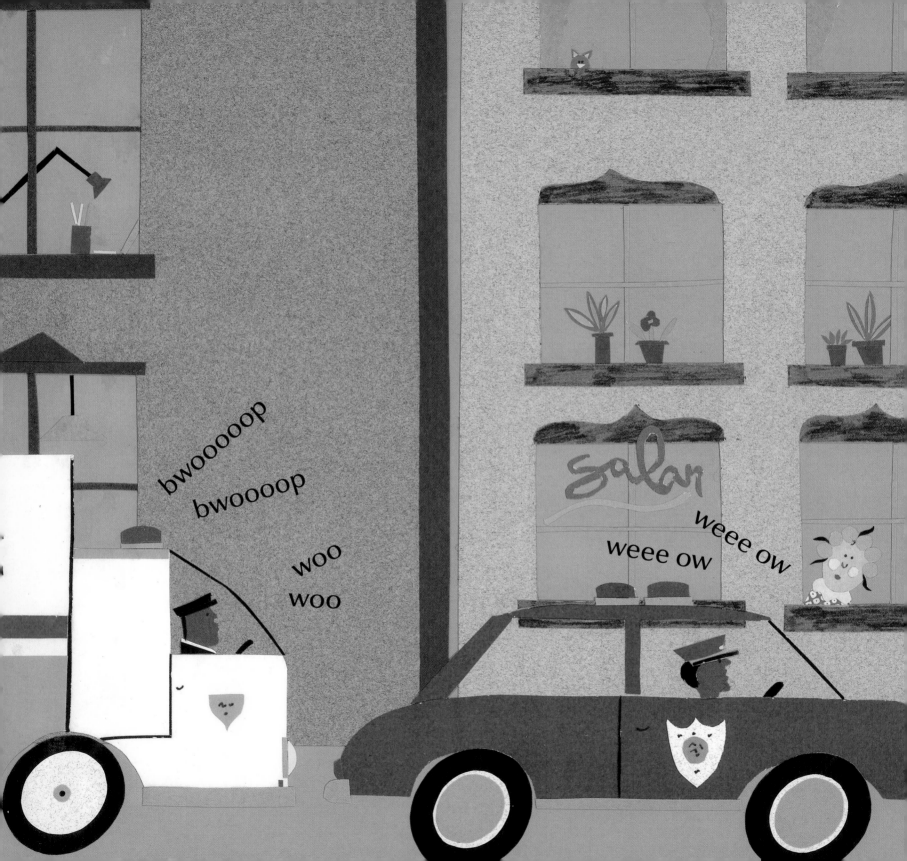

whirrr   clunk   click-a-clack   tip-a-tap   kalunk   kalunk

squeek

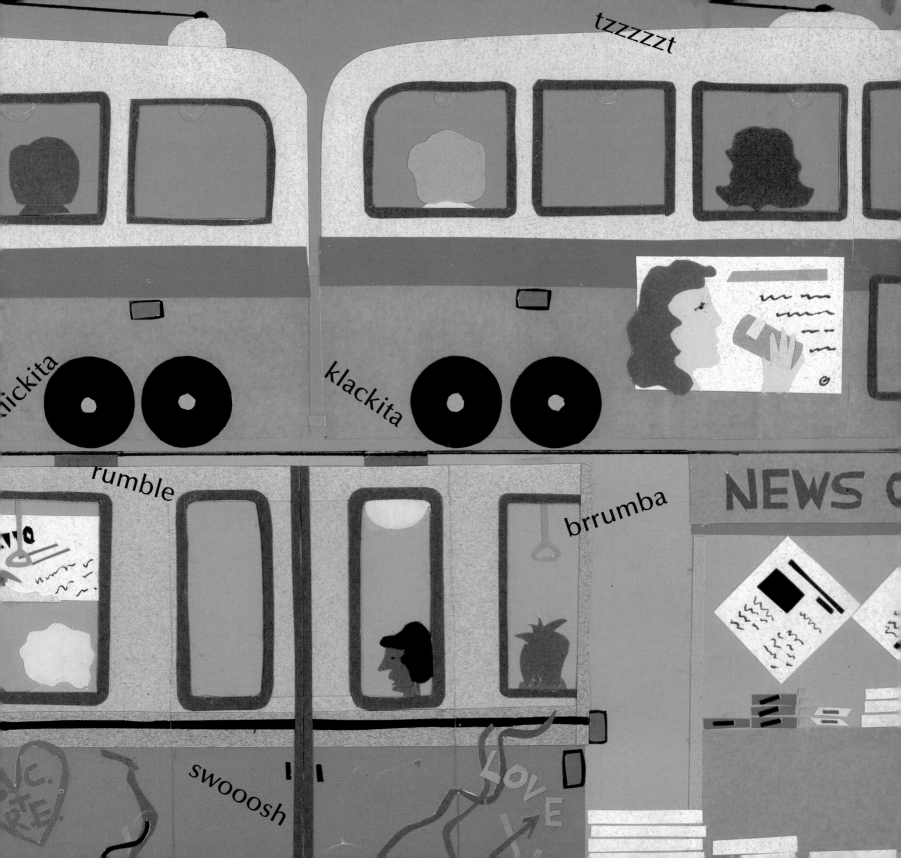

GLOSSARY OF SOUNDS

Here are the sounds that you hear in this book:

Morning sounds

toaster · pop
coffee maker · blip blup
cat · scritch-scratch meow
alarm clocks · birrrrrrr beep beep
snoring · zzzzz
telephone · brrinng brrinng
shower · spisssh lah lah lah
kettle · bweeeet
trash cans · clunk crash

Siren sounds

bwooooop bwooooop
woo wooo
weee ow weee ow
rearrrrrow rearrrrrow
screeeech

Traffic sounds

airplane · zoom
car horns · meep meep beep beep honk honk
trucks · vrooom boop boop screech
drawbridge · ding ding
tug boat · toot toot

Walking sounds

work boots · clump clomp
ballet slippers · pad pad
sneakers · squinch squinch
roller skates · whirrr clunk
boots · click-a-clack
high heels · tip-a-tap
cowboy boots · kalunk kalunk
rats · squeek

Subway and trolley sounds

klickita klackita
rumble rumble
brrumba brrrumba
tzzzzzt tzzzzzt
swooosh

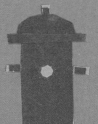

Construction sounds

cement truck · whirrrr

barricade · clik tik

pneumatic drills · rat-a-tat-a-tat

demolition ball · BOOMMM CRASH

bricks · crash clunk

crane · grrrrr

Park sounds

pigeons · coo coo

police whistle · tweet

horse · klip klop

ice-cream cart · ting-a-ling ring-a-ding

squirrel · chirrup

reader · harrump

Radio sounds

dog singing · aroooooo

hey

birrrrr

la la la

bap boom bah boom ba boom

doo wop doo wop doo

bssh bop dee bssh

na na na

dat dah dah

Night sounds

TV · blah blah

popcorn · poppita poppita

cat · yeowl

doorbell · bing bong

burglar alarm · WOOP WOOP WOOP

breaking glass · crack

trash · klang crash

rat · eek

party · klink haha klink blah blah

snoring · zzzzz

smoke alarm · bip bip bip bip

**Can you think of more sounds
you hear in the city?**